A Passion for Innocence

Sex and Sexuality in the Paintings of John Currin

by Henry Berry

Henry Berry is an author of books on modern and postmodern culture as these cultural phases draw in elements of the past, transform these, and in so doing form the grounds for the future. A PASSION FOR INNOCENCE: SEX AND SEXUALITY IN THE PAINTINGS OF JOHN CURRIN follows his previous books THE PROGRESS OF MODERNITY - FROM REVOLUTION TO FADS and LET THERE BE LINKS - THE SOURCES AND NATURE OF INTERNET RELIGION. He is also a reviewer of art books from American and European publishers and nonfiction books on cultural studies, history, and other subjects from university presses. For more than 25 years, he has been active in the interrelated writing and publishing fields as a freelance writer and editor, publishing columnist, publishing consultant for independent publishers and authors, literary agent, and creative writing teacher. He has degrees in philosophy from Fairfield University and Georgetown University. He can be contacted at henryberryinct@gmail.com; or PO Box 176, Southport, CT 06890.

Other Books by the author:

LET THERE BE LINKS - The Sources and Nature of Internet Religion

THE PROGRESS OF MODERNITY - From Revolution to Fads

A PASSION FOR INNOCENCE

SEX AND SEXUALITY IN THE PAINTINGS OF JOHN CURRIN

by Henry Berry

CONTENT

Foreword

For about twenty years now, from about 1990 through 2010, John Currin (b. 1962) has been astutely and in the eyes of many, puzzlingly portraying sweeping changes in the American psyche and American life in the period of highly-developed postmodernism. The sweeping changes are wrought by the changing relationship to innocence that has since the country's origins been at the heart of its identity, ideals, sense of destiny, political activity, and international affairs. Threatened rupture of this relationship to innocence inevitably causes deep psychic discomfort, sense of loss, and worry about the future. All of these and more are reflected in Currin's paintings over the past twenty years.

The paintings can be divided into two distinct groups. The first, early group is paintings roughly in the last decade of the twentieth century; the second, later group, paintings in the first decade of the twenty-first century, with most of these dated in the last years of the decade. The first group begun in the last days of the Reagan presidency and continuing through much of the Clinton presidency reflects the unsettling sense that innocence is slipping away; and this first group depicts the stances, ploys, and artifices resorted to by individuals to deny or try to stave off this. The second group of Currin paintings reflects a reformulated sense of innocence throughout the culture. This reformulation occurred following the 9/11 terrorist attack on the World Trade Towers and as the United States was engaged in large-scale military actions in Iraq and Afghanistan. The traditional sense of innocence relating to the country's origins and founding as a political entity did slip away. But instead of the culture refashioning itself in more seasoned, realistic terms with an objective, reminiscent, and perhaps wistful perspective on innocence, the culture accomplished a thorough reformulation of innocence derived from postmodern sensibilities. The original and originating sense of innocence relating to Puritan religion was replaced by a postmodern sense.

The postmodern sense of innocence involves almost entirely postmodern concepts of sex and sexuality. These concepts inhere in Currin's paintings mostly from about 2008 to 2010. Whereas the traditional relationship with innocence based on the Puritan religion meant to keep innocence in human lives in ways in which this is possible by authority and self-discipline, the relationship with sex and sexuality in postmodern culture is one where these have been assimilated so as to be an essential part of the weave of personal identity and public, cultural experiences and mores. Although the Puritan and the postmodern conceptions of innocence are essentially different, both are inspired and formed by the elemental, primordial human characteristics of sex and sexuality as presented in the vignette of God's banishment of Adam and Eve from Eden in the Book of Genesis; which banishment is commonly seen as a myth about the Fall of Humankind from Paradise. The Puritan regard of sex and sexuality relates to the post-Fall condition of Adam and Eve as representative of Humankind, whereas the postmodern regard relates to their pre-Fall state. Contemporary culture has been drained of last remnants of Puritanism. Nonetheless, it continues to adhere to Christianity in subtly, subconsciously, yet instinctively and determinedly exploring Christianity's paradigmatic creation myth.

"The Passion for Innocence - Sex and Sexuality in the Paintings of John Currin" describes and interprets Currin's paintings from about 1990 through 2010 as collected in two sources. The first of these is the art book "John Currin" published in 2003 by Abrams in conjunction with the Chicago Museum of Contemporary Art and the London Serpentine Gallery where the paintings in the book had been exhibited. The second source is the New York Gagosian Gallery Fall 2010 exhibition of recent Currin paintings. All the paintings discussed in "The Passion for Innocence" are found at various online sites for readers interested in referring to them apart from the descriptions of these in the book.

The two sources used for "The Passion for Innocence" do not exhaust Currin's paintings over his career to date. However, the sources do represent almost completely Currin's characteristic style and variations within it and the artist's range of visual and cultural subjects. Also, the paintings from the sources allow for comparisons of Currin's earlier and later paintings as well as certain continuities and focus of his career. Analysis of individual paintings, comparisons of certain ones, and continuities within the characteristic style and subject matter reveal facets of the passion for innocence in latter-day, highly-refined modern culture that is the interest of this book.

PART ONE: The Fraying of Innocence - 1990's Paintings

1. The Potency of Innocence and the Spectrum of Its Fading

With its association with the blessed world of childhood, a guiltless mind, and immortality, innocence has a extraordinary, preternatural, power on the psyche and behavior. This exceptional, unique power frequently interferes with the natural cycle of innocence from infancy through early adolescence so that an imagined or idealized view of innocence--as if innocence were a "value"--persists beyond its natural presence in human life. Persons resist aging mentally and physically. With many persons, this power of innocence is such that they virtually deny the irrefutable fact of aging and construct virtual worlds in which they are ageless. The preeminence of the "youth market" attests to the power of innocence in the culture. The passion for exercise and related appeal of sports, the sophisticated techniques of cosmetic surgery, popular entertainment, clothing fashions, and car designs and accouterments are all elements of this youth market based on the power of innocence.

This prolonged, lifelong memory of innocence does not always have troublesome and sometimes destructive effects with individuals and society. The common experience of childhood innocence creates a bond among all persons. This experience of innocence is the source of optimism and ideals, without which human life would be flat and colorless. Unfortunately, this same experience of innocence is also the source of totalitarianism and tyranny, which are different kinds of searches for it and attempts to recreate it. For most persons, however, the childhood experience of innocence is a humanizing experience. Throughout later, adult life, the capacious, indefinite memory of this imposes restraints on actions and aims; as most are reluctant to disregard or perhaps lose this memory by indifference or excess, and to threaten or maraud it in others. But Currin's art is not concerned with the salutary effects of innocence. Instead, Currin, a contemporary artist with complex perceptions and inherent reflection, paints varied ways different types of individuals with both generic and individualized attributes mean to be true to the quality and the idea of innocence in a time when globalization is breaking down familiar social and economic relationships and patterns; a steady influx of immigrants with different concepts of the body and different aesthetic tastes is changing the composition of the population; there is prevalent manifest cynicism in the political system and indifference or apathy throughout the public; and there are growing strains among different sectors from stark differences in economic standing and prospects and competing values. The cultural environment, historical events, and political rhetoric and behavior bespeak the loss of innocence.

In his paintings, Currin captures the momentous, multifarious moment when the paucity of innocence is exposed. In the time before this moment, innocence was virtually a spiritual quality shaping action moving into the future and generating expectations of what would be awaiting in this future. More than anything else, it was the sense of innocence igniting enthusiasm for actions and projects. And the sense of innocence, too, was like a blessing that was a sign that these were worthy and investing them with the assurance that they would be accomplished. This sense of innocence, with the satisfying state it formed and the desired future it held out, forestalled any doubt; and blunted any questioning or criticisms from others. The innocence was a mythos--practically a mystique--that was self-perpetuating by a mix of self-image, jingoism, and denial of personal traits or external circumstances implying its diminution or absence.

Denial, delusion, and customs can keep admission of the diminution or evanescence of innocence from formulating and being incorporated into behavior, outlook, or decision. Nonetheless, organic-like as other emotions, moods, and states of being, innocence ineluctably creates traces of the strength and form of its presence and the phases of its ebbing in the self-awareness and senses of individuals and also societies such as the United States that value innocence highly. Such traces cannot help but affect behavior and image. Such effects can range from slight, subtle, practically unnoticeable to overt, symbolic, and ostentatious, even aggressive. The fleeting wince of regret when an older person is reminded of his or her bygone youth upon seeing this displayed in a younger person is one such slight, subtle effect. An older man or woman flagrantly sporting clothing popular with teens is an ostentatious, comical, effect.

Currin's paintings of individual women highlight the relationship between innocence and simplicity. These paintings are themselves simple with their subject of a single individual in a shaded, nondescript background. "Mary O'Connor" (dated 1989) is a typical painting. The subject wears a white blouse, has pale skin and blond hair, an expressionless mouth and eyes; and she is against a background graduated from pale white at the bottom to pale blue at the top. There is nothing pronounced about the woman imparting that she represents a facet of innocence. But this is the point--namely, the mediocrity of innocence. The plainness and simplicity of the woman, along with the plainness and simplicity of the setting, bespeaks the passivity and inwardness of innocence. This passivity and inwardness appeals to the sense of individuality of Americans. These qualities of innocence make innocence feel like a religious sense. It is mostly this sense stirred by the belief in innocence that is referred to when it is said that Americans are among the most religious people in the world.

Other paintings of women from the early 1990s are similar--a single woman with plain features and a plain background. The women are too individualistic to be dismissed. Yet one knows nothing about them because of the plainness of their features, expressions, and clothes, and because of the emptiness of the backgrounds. It is only in the context of the range of Currin's paintings over the preceding fifteen years that one discerns what aspect of innocence he is attempting to divulge as precisely as he can in these early paintings.

The effects of these traces innocence creates are pictured in Currin's paintings. A young girl's confusion over the harbingers of maturity; a middle-aged man's reflex to conceal and hopefully triumph over the nagging intimations of old age; an elderly woman's witless, fearful flaying at the encroachments of infirmity; and the enthused, hapless movements of two virile young men sailing on a boundless ocean all depict different behaviors and signs arising from the mysterious, central presence of innocence and changes in it in individuals. The common thread to these paintings of widely varied individuals and settings is representing an effect of the intuition of the protean, waning nature and the impermanence of innocence. Natural responses--effects--to the sense of the waning of innocence are maturation, wisdom, and fatefulness. But when innocence is idealized mainly for its association with youth, such natural responses are interfered with by confusions, disturbances, fears, and denials, and by willfulness and artifices to cover these over. Individuals do not mature, and do not grow in wisdom. Such resistances to the waning of innocence not only cut individuals off from the natural course of innocence, but also take individuals out of nature. For innocence is such a potent element in human life that efforts to deny its waning and keep it immediate and vital inevitably entail a confused willfulness and stratagems of artificiality.

2. The Restless Eye of Flawed Innocence

Currin creates images of the unseemliness of innocence obsessively desired. Taken as a whole, Currin's paintings mostly of modern-day individuals and couples are a comment on a desire for innocence that remains at the heart of American society. This innocence persists well after the point when it should have at least been tempered by experience. Whether self-consciously forced to conform to mythology of America as the New World or reflexively resorted to in the absence of worldly, complex perceptions of the environment and oneself, the innocence exerts a power independent of the diversity of the physical world, the tensions of history, the balances of society, and the mysteries of person. Whether act of will or witless measure, innocence comes upon the scene simplifying everything--relationships, questions, doubts, past, present, future. Innocence is posited by pose or held out by reflex as the ground for common humanity that virtually blots out any differences and with this any suspicions, reservations, or doubts. This is the presumed power of innocence with its simplicity, pureness, and wholeness.

Currin pictures different sides of this compulsive, disruptive innocence from its ready, sweet manifestation, to its determined projection, to its communal, liberating, yet ultimately confining fabrication. Svelte blond-haired adolescent girls belie the fatal flaw in the presumed innocence. The titles of two 1995 paintings are "Girl on a Hill" and "SuperAngel." The title "Girl on a Hill" seems innocence enough; and even the hyperbolized

"SuperAngel" is not patently ironic or dismissive considering its subject is an attractive young girl. The young girl of each painting is sitting on a hillside. Each girl is dressed simply, one in a dress and the other in a shirt and jeans. The hair of each reaches to about the middle of her back. Besides the young girl, there is the foliage of the hillside and a blue sky with fair-weather clouds. In each painting, frail golden-haired girls sitting peacefully on gentle slopes beneath fair skies suggest the aura and eternity of innocence. Yet the girl of each painting discloses the innocence is flawed in self-consciously looking out of the painting toward the viewer. Innocence is absorbing. It is not absorbing in such a way that it blocks out the world, as a rejection or critique of it. Innocence does not have such mechanisms. Innocence is absorbing in such a way that it issues its own world.

Innocence is not aware of the common, fallen world. Fulfilling and sustaining on its own, innocence does not look toward others. Every element of Currin's paintings of the adolescent girls--their wide eyes, their gently sloped shoulders, the peaceful setting, the colors--goes into a picture of innocence. But the girls' looking out toward the viewer discloses that the innocence is flawed. It no longer has even the potency to induce reverie in a patently peaceful setting. Without reverie nurtured by innocence, individuals have no source for conceiving a better self or ideals. The young girls of the paintings are too young to have a consciousness of what is amiss since the innocence is flawed. Their behavior, however, reveals they in some way sense something is not right. They look around to try to become aware of what is amiss.

The girls embody innocence. But with the innocence flawed, there is no continually refreshed, coherent inner life. Thus, the girls turn outward. The innocence the girls embody is the flawed, elusive, vaguely distressing innocence of contemporary life.

3. The Shared Abortive Search for Innocence

Whereas the girls, in the ingenuousness of adolescence, show their sense of a flawed, disappointing, innocence by turning outward, older persons in other of Currin's paintings attempt to disguise a much-diminished innocence by the formality of poses. The man-and-woman couples in "Lovers in the Country" (1993) and "The Neverending Story" (1994) are focused on an innocence that is apart from their relationship. The marked difference in the ages of the younger women and older men as well as dressy, somewhat showy or theatrical clothing of the men suggest the conventional delusion that appearances or association with youth can bring back a departed innocence. The golden hair of the men and the golden hair of the woman in "Lovers in the Country" also go toward the intonation of a bygone golden age. In the "Lovers in the Country," the dark patch of the man's double-breasted sport jacket contrasts with the spots of gold.

What comes out beyond any details and implications in both paintings is the stiffness of the poses of the men. Their shoulders and arms are angular. They peer intently at some unseen point out of the paintings. Unlike the adolescent girls, the men do not look at the viewer; but rather they look to the left. Though relatively natural in their poses, the woman too are involved in the attempt to bring innocence into the relationship. The couples believe that innocence is meant to be a part of a relationship; that a central purpose of a relationship is innocence. The men attach themselves to the younger women in the expectation that youth holds innocence. The women attach themselves to the men in the belief that age knows how to find innocence. But by their vaguely tortured poses, the characters in the paintings reveal their sense that their beliefs are errant. However, they do not know what else to do. In a culture where youth is celebrated and fetishized, the comfort of wisdom and grace isolate one.

4. The Flight from Infirmity

Currin's painting "The Cripple" (1997) is one other one which represents especially his insight that the inevitably fruitless search for lost innocence gives rise to artifice and insincerity. The title denotes what Currin wants the viewer to see chiefly about the woman in the painting. Besides the title, to emphasize this basic subject, the woman's left hand clasps the curved top of a cane in front of her left hip. Except for part of the woman's hand wrapped around its curved top binding the hand to the cane, the cane is the closest aspect of the painting to the viewer. The woman's air jars with the title and the conspicuous sign of her infirmity. With her left shoulder thrust forward jauntily and her openmouthed smile, the woman presents a breezy manner. Going along with these affects, her right hand, misshapen and appearing to be missing the two fingers away from the thumb, is placed on her right hip with the right elbow obviously jutting out like the left shoulder even though the elbow is not seen. In addition, the woman's long hair is blown out toward the left, as if by a breeze.

There is nothing about the woman's manner--her appearance--which indicates she acknowledges that she is crippled. Since the woman carries a cane, she shows she is aware of her infirmity. But she has not assimilated the fact of her infirmity so that it has affected either her manner or her psyche. She has to use the cane. But this can be minimized to the degree that it is practically denied by a jaunty spirit and a quick, openmouthed smile.

The hair flying away from the head and the outward thrusts of the shoulder and the elbows convey the woman putting distance between herself and her infirmity. She is not trying to escape it altogether--she knows she needs her cane. But as the sharp angles of the elbows and shoulders are like fences and corners meant to remove the infirmity from sight, they also represent the woman's blindness and self-deceptions by which she keeps the infirmity at a distance. The woman is suppressing full, life-changing realization of her infirmity. She is not trying to escape awareness of it. She cannot deny the necessity of the cane. But her appearance is not alarmed or embarrassed by this diversion she engages in. Besides being like fences and corners putting the infirmity out of sight, her shoulder and elbows hint at a certain determination to ignore the infirmity. In this, they relate to the determined, though ultimately futile, poses of the men in the paintings of the couples.

Like the men, the woman has not developed a pathological or ineffectual--or a dislikable--character despite the artifices and errancy of her manner. They have a cogency, as willed and misplaced as it may be. The determination of the men makes for their cogency. With the woman, it is her smile.

It is the smile mostly which gives the woman the air of breeziness. Without the smile, the determination hinted at in the angular shoulders and elbows would be overt, as in the serious gazes and set poses of the men. But the smile of the woman renders the shoulders and elbows something more than only signs of determination. The smile renders the elbows and shoulders actors in the jauntiness, props in the cogency the woman has put together to keep the infirmity at a distance while managing to be effective in her actions and mentally balanced.

The woman has not assimilated her infirmity; it is kept at a distance by a combination of breeziness keeping it from settling into the person of the woman and the tactic of preemption of it as a point requiring any consideration by a large, quick smile accompanying the image of vitality and control projected by the breeziness.

5. Different Factors of Different Relationships to Innocence

The men and the women have different relationships to innocence. But both are constructed relationships, sophisticated despite their errancy and futility. The men look outward for an innocence they imagine beckons them.

For their relationship with the younger women testifies to the reality of this innocence. As is clear from the younger woman's postures and expressions, they are involved with the men because they share with them the belief in innocence. Each woman looks to the respective man to preserve and also strengthen the innocence shared by the couple. The men believe that by possessing the innocence they seek as an element of the outward world, they will fulfill themselves, in large part by justifying the younger women's attraction to them.

The men's relationship to innocence is a delusion inspired by ambitions of eternal youth, dreams of everlasting sexual vigor, and fantasies of transcending the tolls of time. The relationship to innocence Currin depicts in his paintings of the couples involves stereotypical traits of men and women, the symbiotic reinforcement of the belief in innocence, the idea that innocence is a communal asset, and how behavior and relationships are affected by and structured by the assumption of innocence. The couples represent the social dimension of the American belief in innocence.

The couples portray both the stiltedness and the fragility in relationships where innocence has a significant place. Currin's distortions and exaggerations illustrate this stiltedness and fragility. The stiltedness can make a relationship--or a society--seem special. And the fragility can give a sense of poignancy. The sense of specialness and the poignancy are the sweet fruits of innocence. They are the reasons for its allure; the helpless pursuit of it; and the deceptions and subterfuges which keep the sense of innocence fresh and the belief in it whole and accessible.

But the sense of specialness and of poignancy are momentary. For the sense of specialness is hedonistic. And the poignancy is a nostalgia. More deeply, these keep individuals from true knowledge of one another, from the lessons of experience, and from consciousness of the ambiguous balances and undeniable, unalterable workings of the world.

The affluence of the couples (implied by their clothing and their general appearance), their health, the innocence they see in each another or at least the capacity of the other to awaken or inflate it they see, and their vulnerabilities which seek innocence as a balm give them the belief that innocence is a part of the world, like a garden or a sunrise or a horizon. The woman of Currin's "The Cripple", with her infirmity, has an overt, discernible, relationship with innocence which is an integral, material part of American life too. Her relationship is complex; although not so complex as that of the couples' since it does not involve so many variables (e. g., the fluid psyches and weaves of experience of more than one person) and its bounds are confined to herself. The relationship of the couples to innocence is basically a mythic relationship with political and sociological effects. The woman's relationship, on the other hand, is restricted to herself; even though it is frequently played out in various social interchanges. The primary difference in the relationships with innocence is that the couples' implies distinctive ideals and visions of America; whereas the woman's is a strategy--albeit one derived from the dominating American vision of innocence--for psychic health and social acceptance. Because of this fundamental, for the most part radical, difference, the dynamic and results of the relationship to innocence are different in the two relationships.

The trick for the couples for keeping the belief in innocence vibrant and accessible is assimilating the historical and traditional idea of innocence into their lives as they grow and participate in varied, interconnected parts of American society. This assimilation occurs by ceremonies, political rhetoric, education, and moral instruction in families, schools, and churches. With individuals, the assimilation occurs by a subtle, yet strong resistance to the unfinished lessons cast up by the ambivalent flow and episodes of experience. The resistance keeps the individual whole, youthful (or youth-like in many ways), and ever open to transformation and renewal, but at the expense of orderly, grounded, dependable, wisdom-filled maturation. This resistance running throughout American culture recurringly becomes manifest in ways ranging from space exploration and overseas adventures to youthful clothing and cosmetic surgery. Such corporate and overt aspects of innocence are insinuated and represented by the couples in the Currin paintings. The resistance to experience and maturation which is key to keeping innocence fresh and accessible is portrayed particularly in the awkward stiffness of the poses of the men and in the childlike expressions and girlish postures of the women. In American culture, such willed poses and simple appearances have become practically iconic for their evocation of innocence. Such willfulness as is contained in the poses is seen as verifying that innocence is readily accessible, like a reflex; and ingenuous appearance imparts that innocence is vibrant so a to be affective and cleansing.

In contrast to the couples, the relationship of the woman in the painting "The Cripple" to innocence has been stricken by the brute fact of her infirmity. The couples present a dreamy regard of innocence from being persuaded to acknowledge it by the country's mores even though they sense that it is unreal. The woman has a sharp sense of innocence because she is in danger of losing her sense of it, whether it is real or not.

To lose one's sense of innocence in American society is to be a pariah. The woman's effort to keep herself whole despite her infirmity is at the same time an effort to remain within the ambient of American society. With her conspicuous and undeniable infirmity, the woman has slipped into a fallen world, a world of injury, struggle, pain, and limitations. She is no longer able to take part in the Edenic New World of successive new beginnings. With her infirmity, her task is to minimize as much as possible-- almost to the point of denial--her infirmity which is a glaring rejoinder to society of the impossibility of unaffected innocence. Since her infirmity cannot be removed or hidden, her task is basically one of keeping up appearances, of keeping up the appearance of unaffected innocence as much as this is possible. Hence, the smile she projects with the intention of distracting others from her infirmity.

With her smile, she tries to communicate to others that her infirmity which could be seen as an insult to innocence does not weigh on her; nor has it affected her belief in the reality, accessibility, desirability, and preeminence of innocence. If she does not recognize her infirmity as changing anything significant about her relationship to innocence, why should anyone else? In fact, by not letting her infirmity which might have disillusioned her about innocence affect her relationship to innocence in any meaningful way, she implicitly presents herself as a paradigmatic testament to the strength of the hold of innocence in the psyche of the countless members of society. Along with her smile intended to distract others from her infirmity, her splayed, windmill-like limbs are like semaphore flags sending the message that the infirmity is to be only barely acknowledged, if the angular, energetic limbs do not manage to virtually obscure it entirely.

Whereas the couples represent a dreamlike state where the society's myth of innocence meets elemental psychic needs, the woman by contrast engages in a struggle to keep the reality of her infirmity from working its way into the depths of her psyche and bringing changes in demeanor and movement other than those which are forced upon her. Whereas the relationship with innocence of the affluent, well-to-do couples is dreamy, the relationship of the women is existential. She cannot deny her infirmity, a plain physical fact. With any dream of innocence burst, the best she can now do is attempt to distract attention from her infirmity as best she can and put out signs that what cannot be denied by her or others has not affected her fundamentally, and will not be allowed to repudiate either her or other's belief in innocence. However much the woman may have made mental adjustments because of her infirmity, basically she is struggled to remain a member in good standing of society. For she will find little sympathy or even understanding of the effects of infirmity in the restless, quixotic American society. Besides picturing the gestures and manner of the struggle to hang on to the belief in innocence, Currin's painting "The Cripple," with its stiff, angular arms and unfounded, drifting smile, pictures as well the desperation of one engaged in this struggle.

The couples and the woman of Currin's paintings analyzed above represent different angles on the belief in innocence central to American society. These paintings depict and implicate comparatively complex relationships. In the paintings of the couples, the relationship has become relatively complex by the women's looking to the men for confirmation of innocence. The men do not assume any role of the mature male or fatherly figure, but instead play to the younger women's desire for innocence. In "The Cripple," the relationship has become relatively complex by the woman's infirmity. She has to somehow confirm by her own resources the continuing presence of innocence. But practically all of Currin's paintings can be viewed as representing different facets of the relationship to innocence in American life.

6. The Haven of Homosexuality

Currin's 1990's paintings portray the varied ways people are responding to the inchoate, though ineluctable erosion of the traditional, historical, formative belief in innocence. These ways varied from affectless, nearly mindless presentation of self; the unprompted, spontaneous excitement of adolescent women; the posturing and anticipations of couples of an older man and younger woman; the magic-like tricks of older women to distract from the realities of age and infirmity; the awkwardness and evasions in a klatch in suburbia; to gays taking excessive, soporific pleasure in mundane scenes and shared affections. In the 1990s, Currin could not move beyond such portrayals because ones sensing the ineluctable erosion were not moving beyond such fragmentary, seemingly jejune and incongruous response. Currin the artist is not a visionary, prophet, or healer. Currin the artist is a social observer. He could not get ahead of the social phenomena stirring his artistic skills and interests.

Currin's presentations of how the ineluctable erosion of the founding sense of innocence would be resolved by the culture are seen in his early twenty-first century paintings, particularly ones from 2009 and 2010. By then, the culture would fully and overtly accomplish its resolution for the erosion by reformulating and accordingly displaying a different, new conception of sex and sexuality which nonetheless still allowed for attachment to innocence. However, presages of this eventual resolution are seen among Currin's 1990's paintings. The portrayals of homosexual couples in the earlier paintings are one such subject, one such presentiment.

Two paintings from the 1990's group exemplify Currin's typical treatment of homosexuality at this time. The two paintings are "Homemade Pasta" (1999) and "Two Guys" (2002, nevertheless patently going with the 1990's paintings)

"Homemade Pasta" pictures a homosexual couple making pasta in a kitchen. The individuals look into the shared activity of churning long strands of pasta out of a pasta-maker. In the background are three shelves. But rather than being filled with ordinary kitchen or household objects, they are mostly empty. Two wine glasses, a short stack of five plates, a pie plate, and a rumpled towel are widely scattered across the shelves. With only bare surrounding, enclosing background, the homosexual pair seem adrift, with their calm, intent, pleased faces seeming to look for too much pleasure, too much reinforcement, too much evenness and emotional ground in this commonplace, mechanical domestic activity. Nonetheless, the contentment is genuine, if transient and maybe not even reproducible. The homosexual pair are not untouched by the anxieties and stresses of the disturbances in the relationship with innocence and inevitable repercussions on notions of sex and sexuality. With their homosexuality, however, they pass through these with an equilibrium and ability for whole, satisfactory emotional experiences and moments as modest as these might be which the heterosexual couples are unable to find.

Two Guys" is a simpler painting in which two ordinary-looking men sit in a simple embrace facing the viewer. A brown-haired man with relatively short neat hair wearing a brown-gold shirt is a little higher than the other, as if sitting on the next higher row of bleacher seats. The second man who is a little forward in the painting sits back between the knees and thighs of the first's legs spread open with feet on the (presumed) bench-like seat the second sits on. The brown-haired man's arms lightly drape the upper body of the second man, who has neatly parted and combed silver-gray hair and a neat mustache and w ears a white t-shirt. The right arm of the second man rests on the right thigh of the first man. The closer man's left arm drops out of sight held against his left side. The men's embrace is affectionate, not sexual. They could be brothers just casually sitting together, or close cousins. One ascribes homosexuality to them mainly in the context of Currin paintings, particularly the way it compares to the ordinariness of the homosexual pair in "Homemade Pasta."

The most notable feature of "Two Guys" is the naturalness of the light embrace of the two men. In "Two Guys," any implication of the edginess, flamboyance, or unconventionality of homosexuality usually conveyed by images of homosexual sex or sexuality is absent. In fact, the naturalness and comfortableness of the two men with each other is not found in any Currin paintings of men and women couples. The older men and younger women couples of "Lovers in the Country" and "The Neverending Story" have a stilted relationship as evidenced by their poses and somewhat hopeful, yet unnerved gazes. By the simplicity of the image of the relationship and the comfort the homosexual couple find in it and in each other in the paintings "Homemade Pasta" and "Two Guys," Currin implies that homosexuality is a haven for the harsh conflicts and subversive concerns of sex and sexuality overcoming individuals and their relationships. In Currin paintings of the following decade, the homosexuality formerly presented as a haven transforms into an aspect of the resolution for the conflicts and concerns of sex and sexuality.

7. An Ensemble of Awkwardness

One of Currin's most complex and insightful paintings, "Stamford After-Brunch" (2000) pictures three thirtyish women sitting closely together on a sofa. The women on the left and the right who are more into the foreground than the middle one hold half-full martini glasses. All three hold small unlit cigars. Stamford is a city in Connecticut, but the setting is not urban, but suburban. The women are on a sofa in a comfortable suburban home as indicated by the fine flower-patterned cover of the large sofa holding them, the rounded part of a piano in the left middle ground, the large, many-paneled window past the piano, and outside of this, bare trees with snow on their limbs and on the ground. (Although Stamford is a city, it is a part of the greater New York City suburban area with country-like areas of large homes with large, landscaped yards.)

Nonetheless, the women would most likely be recognized as suburban women without the background features from their costly clothing (giving off a sheen) and the behavior they are engaged in. The women show no sophistication as evident by their postures, expressions and mixed faint sense of glee and sense of acting out a trivial, routine transgression--really, little more than a faux pas--of having a drink early in the day and, for women, smoking cigars, or at least in this case thinking about it. The middle women is not shown to be holding a martini glass. Her hand that is pictured holds an unlit cigar. The left and right women clink their glasses as if in a ceremonial toast which is close to the center of the painting.

Both of them hold unlit cigars. But the one on the left holds hers not with her finger tips as if she could draw from it if it were lit: she holds it--more cradles it--between the index and middle fingers of her right hand so that smoking it would be tricky or impossible because of the interference of her knuckles. Adding to the women's realization that they are not really engaged in any transgression to speak of, they are not looking at one another as this is often a part of a shared experience and can affirm the significance or meaning of it. The eyes of the middle woman and the one on the right are at least half-closed and possibly lightly fully-closed. With their small cigars held at about chin level, it appears they could be casting their eyes at these. However, the amount of eyelid shown above the lashes indicates they aren't looking at the cigars; although as part of the routine of the at best barely transgressive scene, they are imagining they are. The woman of the left has her eye which is shown in the profile of her head half open in what looks like a weak squint. With eye socket dark with no hint of a pupil, she is plainly not visually taking in the scene nor much involved or interested in it.

The most noticeable feature of "Stamford After-Brunch" is the postures of the women on the left and right leaning toward one another as they clink glasses in the space between them. But practically every other detail of the figures or associated with them--unlit cigars, clinking glasses instead of drinking from them, disinterested eyes, weak connection to what they are engaged in, no sign of any connection or communication among them other than their sitting close to one another and the assumption they are friends--works against the ordinary, conventional impression, assumption, or symbol that two individuals leaning toward one another in such a domestic setting are meaning to commune with one another in the atypical proceedings and reverie of the moment. Currin builds tensions, contradictions, and perplexities into the painting by an assembly of details countervailing to the primary impression. The women are not trying to trick one another by their poses of involvement and handling of the objects of the scene. With the cunning of a chess master and the social awareness of a consummate public relations or advertising whiz, Currin is depicting something other than this. He is depicting the fissures in the integrity of personality and cracks in the structure and playing out of social interaction and ritual revealing instabilities in these.

The women of the scene of "Stamford After-Brunch" are mustering through a shared, somewhat manufactured moment looking for something rather than participating fully in it or even willingly in any meaningful sense. The details of the closed or vacant eyes, the misheld cigar, and others indicating they are distanced from the enactment even though physically present and performing the appropriate acts suggest they are drawn into themselves-- perhaps scouring their memory for similar past incidents whose recollection would inform them of why they are going though this one of the moment; perhaps some surviving quality or interest which explains or justifies the banality of the drinks and cigars; perhaps the undeniable realization that any such quality or interest is past and gone for good, and thus any such moment is bound to be dissatisfying, futile, and falsified. The anomalies and the waywardness of features of the women in the painting depict an emotional honesty which has not yet consciously entered into mentality so that it informs behavior and can be articulated.

Not only are the Stamford women not trying to trick one another, they are not trying to trick the viewer either. The clues for what is going on are evident. And if these were not enough, there are plain, though not blatant, deformations to the bodies of the two women in the foreground. The neck of the woman on the left (the one with the vacant eyes) is unnaturally elongated (a feature repeated by Currin in other paintings). Rather than suggest that as part of her body reaching into the center of the scene to partake more of it (as if "craning" her neck), along with the other anomalies, this deformation communicates a crack in the familiarity of the women and the setting. The other hypothetical physical deformation (too odd to be true) is the much exaggerated rump of the woman on the right. As the elongation of the neck of the woman on the left suggests a forced, unnatural, effort to take part in the group scene, the bulging, hefty rump of the woman on the right suggests that she is being kept from partaking of the scene. Though the angle of her back leading into the center of the scene and the placement of her hands in the center (like features of the woman on the left) are directed toward the center where the activity is occurring, the rumpled, coarse, bulging rump seems like a weight or alternate center of gravity tugging at her and expressing her reservations and questions about the enactment. Unnaturally elongated neck near the center. Exaggerated, bulging rump at the periphery of the circle of the women. Anomalous details. Currin paints not a trompe l'oeil, but a trompe l'esprit.

8. The Empty Bucket

"The Gardeners" is another Currin painting where individuals--in this case, a husband and wife--are presented almost as in relief against a spare, neutral background. This minimal place of a background tells that Currin means for the concentration to be on individuals in his paintings. Currin is not concerned about biography, social standing, talismans of identity, nor self-image as this can be deduced from public appearance. He is concerned about cultural and historical fault lines which are coming under stress and in many cases buckling. The incongruities and anomalies of the paintings are like the fault lines. What appears as the puzzle or strangeness of the individuals is their reflection of the stresses and the buckling.

"The Gardeners" (2001) at 52" by 75" one of Currin's largest paintings has at its center an older married couple apparently engaged in planting something in the ground. Panoramic in its width, the background is nonetheless still sparse and routine. To the left is a panel of a white fence. There are two long-handled shovels, one leaning against the fence, the handle of the other laid across the freshly-dug hole for the planting. In the background beyond the left shoulder of the woman are a luxury car possibly a Jaguar from its sporty, low shape and long hood; and beyond this a large, mansion-like house. In the foreground to the woman's left is the trunk of a tree. The center of the painting is the couple kneeling with both handling a brick-colored pot. Both wear work clothes including gloves and hats; although the woman's hat with a satin sash circling its brim appears a little too fancy.

Closer viewing reveals the pot held between the couple is empty. So is the freshly-dug hole. There is no planting going on. The gardeners are going through the motions (like the women of "Stamford After-Brunch"). Oddities in this painting are the outsized glove worn by the man on his right hand and the article on the woman's left hand which is the same color and pattern as the man's glove but has no fingers and droops over the rim of the empty brick-colored pot. It looks more like a dish rag she wrapped around her hand, or some covering as if the hand is misshapen. There is no renewal which such a scene ordinarily symbolizes, but only an empty ritual of renewal.

9. The Fishermen

The 2002 painting titled "Fishermen" goes with Currin's paintings from his earlier years because it presents a facet of the distressing, confused circumstances rather than an image of the resolution. Nonetheless, it is a big step from these earlier paintings in that the backs of the two nude men are shown; and with this, the backs of their heads. Their faces are not shown. In those few earlier pictures of Currin's where the single individual or two persons were not facing forward as if in a portrait, their faces were still a part of the painting. (The only exception to this is the painting "Twenty-three Years Ago"--1995--where a young adult man and woman are kissing on a hillside. Yet even in this exception, the simple, unitary nature of innocence is represented by the focus of the man and woman on one another.)

Not only the backs of the men in the same vibrant glow as the flesh of the nude women in earlier paintings, but also their gestures, the setting, and symbolisms of the painting invoke innocence, though a different facet, indeed a different dimension of innocence. The two nude men are on a small skiff in choppy waters. The perspective of the painting is such that it appears they are heading into a pale blue sky with high thin clouds. This appearance is reinforced by the gesture of the man to the left: holding one end of a length of rope (about seven feet long), his left hand reaches up and out to the sky. The other end of the rope is held in his right hand which is out from his side and slightly behind him.

There are religious, particularly Christian, intonations to the painting. Although the two nude men are presumed to be homosexuals (a couple of Currin's earlier paintings were of homosexual couples), they could also be seen as apostles of Jesus from some of the other imagery. The miracle of Christ walking on the water comes immediately to mind from the bunch of fish in the middle of the skiff, to the right of the man on the right. The fish are presumably a catch of fish since the man on the right holds a net above him as if to cast it out into the choppy waters. Jesus said to Peter, the head apostle, that Peter was to be a "fisher of men." In the upper left corner of the painting is a seagull. But the seagull has the form of the dove often used to symbolize Jesus. Its wings are outstretched. All of the details of the painting "Fisherman" and its overall impression unmistakably relate to Christianity. An essential aspect of Christianity is the innocence of Jesus Christ, and innocence as a primary virtue. This innocence of Christianity colors all of its religiosity and distinguishes it from other religions. For true Christians, the innocence sanctifies Christianity and raises it above other religions, giving Christians especially the inspiration, justification, and confidence to try to convert others to Christianity.

With its evident references to Christianity, "Fishermen" shifts the consideration of innocence from its psychological and emotional affects on an individual or a couple to the spiritual or idealistic pursuit to attain innocence. The faces of the men are not shown so the viewer cannot read anything into them with respect to the affects innocence has on them as individuals. By its vibrant colors, outward reaching gestures of the men, and the background of the open sky, the painting entails the hopefulness, capaciousness, and promises going with innocence.
Yet, despite the shift in the consideration of innocence and the impressions of its unique, extraordinary spiritual qualities, the painting nonetheless comments on the errancy and delusion of the belief in and pursuit of innocence. This note ties it in with Currin's previous paintings.

Despite the outward gestures of the men and the enthusiasm of their pursuit of innocence as imparted by their robust flesh, the agitation of the water, and the depths and spaciousness of the sky, there are definite signs related directly to them which repeat Currin's view about the limitations and hollowness of misplaced innocence and the perversions the reflexive, customary pursuit of it brings to mentality and behavior. The rope the man on the left holds in his hands is a short length of rope whose purpose is unclear. A length of rope is not out of place with a small boat. But a rope is usually tied to something to secure it, or is handy on a hook or in a storage space to use as needed, to tie the boat to a dock for instance. The man on the left, however, is holding one end of the rope out to the sky. He appears to be making an offering of it to the sky; or he could be meaning, as if in a ritual, to symbolize tying the two men and their boat to the sky, the open, endless sky. But since the rope is not attached to anything, the gesture seems arbitrary and empty; more theatrical than deft or ritualistic. Besides, the notion of "roping" the sky is patently inane. As the sky is associated with innocence--the innocence the men are trying to attain--the inappropriateness of the rope discloses a failure to grasp the nature of innocence.

The man on the right evinces the same clumsy hopefulness as the one of the left. Instead of a rope, this man holds a net above his head. His left hand reaching above his head cocked at a ninety-degree angle at its elbow grips a spot on the edge of the loosely-woven net. The man's right arm reaching across his front at about the height of his neck grips another part of the net. There is no position or motion of the net however so that it can be cast out to the water. If it were cast from the man as it is positioned, it would catch his head in it. And if it were let loose as it is, it would fall draping over the man. The position of the man's arms and the position of the net indicates that the net cannot be cast to the water without much rearrangement of the man's hands and body and of the net. It looks more like the man would pull the net around his shoulders, as one spreads a shawl to wrap around one.

The man on the right is as feckless as the one on the left. The are on a voyage to nowhere in a boundless sea. What hopes and optimism they have are communicated by their bare skin, energized arms, and heading of their skiff into the open sea. With their exposure to the elements and setting off into a boundless sea, the two men--taken to be homosexual--venture further than any other characters of Currin's early group of paintings to search for resolution of the discomforts and uncertainties coming with the changing relationship to innocence. It is evident they are unable to come to any resolution. Nonetheless, the men's large patches of bare flesh taking up the central part of the painting and the painting's seemingly incidental religious symbols and references hold the resolution; which resolution will be related in Currin's following group of paintings.

PART TWO: Innocence Reformulated - The Gagosian Gallery Exhibition, Fall 2010

1. The Emergence of the True Image

In the Fall 2010, the Gagosian Gallery in New York City held an exhibition of about twelve of Currin's newest paintings. With dates of 2009 and 2010, these paintings were done about two decades after the first of Currin's paintings (as presented in the art book "John Currin," Abrams, 2003). While the paintings are unmistakably recognized as Currin works for their bold figures, teasingly scandalous subjects, and occasional limited distortions, the exhibition paintings as a whole and most individually evidence a movement from the paintings of the earlier period.

To begin with, all of the paintings except one are women. And none is a domestic scene. Gone is the play on bourgeois activities and scenes such as in "Stamford After-Brunch" and "The Gardeners." There is not even a tease on common domesticity as with the pair of contented homosexuals cranking out pasta in "Homemade Pasta." Nor does Currin intersperse simple portraits of known persons or types such as an elderly woman or a professorial man.

In the recent paintings shown at the Gagosian Gallery, Currin moves beyond the parameters of his earlier paintings, as wide and loosely-defined as these were. He is no longer much interested in working in enigmatic details. Although there are details in most of the paintings, these do not have the incongruent, anomalous, or perplexing quality of details of earlier paintings. The reason for this is that the later paintings are frank. Having reached a plateau which he was always moving toward, Currin now dispenses with certain touches and techniques so that the true image shines forth. While Currin has never been reserved in display nor circumspect in statement, the details and techniques of his previous paintings making for a complexity and perplexity of them appear now to be way stations for the artist along his road to the plateau he has now arrived at. As such, they were as much securities for the artist as they were oddities and perplexities for the viewer. Not knowing just what he was being moved as an artist to represent, Currin placed incongruities in his paintings to imbue them with ambiguity and perplexity. This served to draw attention from the fact that, as Currin knew, he was not getting an image just the way he wanted it despite his extraordinary skill as an artist and acumen as a social observer.

Notably, Currin has assimilated the latter-day open acceptance of homosexuality (including lesbianism) into certain paintings, and also the general appearance of more explicit sexual (e. g., more flesh exposed) and sexually suggestive imagery in films, TV programs, advertising, and other media. Considering this about Currin's latest paintings with 2009 and 2010 dates, it thus should be no surprise that in February 2011 a Northwestern University professor named J. Michael Bailey allowed a performance of a woman attempting to work herself to orgasm using an electric dildo in an extracurricular, optional class relating to his course named Human Sexuality. (About 160 of 600 students enrolled showed up.) As an artist, Currin is a deft, prescient social critic. The incident at Northwestern affirms his prescience as a social observer, and illustrates how his art work parallels social developments even if it is seen as eccentric, aberrant, inherently self-negating, or excessively and only stylized.

With the wider acceptance, presence, and openness of homosexuality and sexual imagery which is to some degree transformative for society, Currin's paintings are no longer provisional--with the ambiguity and mystique inherent in this--or off-putting or complicated. Rid of their enigmatic details leaving them inscrutable and presenting simpler images rather than complex tableaus or sociological suggestions (e. g., homosexuality can be bourgeois), the paintings have a freshness; which freshness, one sees now, was always inherent in Currin's paintings, but garbled because of their oddities and the artist's unresolved regard of the personality or social scene he was painting.

Although odd, enigmatic details are gone in the later paintings shown at the Gagosian, the characteristic stylistic elements of contorted and somewhat exaggerated features remain. In these later paintings, however, emptied of oddities of detail and puzzled point of view, these stylistic elements largely account for the paintings' freshness. Whereas in the earlier paintings, contortions telegraphed confusion, if not some pain, of a figure, and a degree of falsified appearance or involvement, in the following period of paintings, similar contortions express full, free acquiescence to presentation or participation. Whereas in the earlier paintings, contortions convey uncertainty and a mood of withdrawal reflecting an individual's inner conflict because of changing mores, in the later paintings, such contortions express a glad, overflowing presence or participation. Similarly, the exaggerations no longer appear as if deformities suggesting in their stylistic way conflict and artifice, but now like the contortions, express fullness and pleasure in presentation or participation.

The difference is that the early contortions represented self-protective measures a figure was taking as the inner conflict occurred and the confusion was running its course, where the later contortions communicate an acceptance of openness and desire to share. And where the early exaggerations looking like deformities were like centers of gravity keeping a painting from forming into a single, coordinated image, the later exaggerations are focal points drawing all a painting's parts together and conveying the special delight of a figure. Thus in the number of 2010 exhibition paintings of a range of characters and settings, there are no paintings of figures such as the married couple in "The Gardeners" (2001) with their faces only partly visible and mostly shrouded in large hats they wear as engaged in their task. In the later paintings, fresh-looking faces are consistently fully visible. In one painting, "Hotpants" (2010), showing a homosexual dandy sporting a pair of thigh-high shorts, Currin has him looking into a full-length mirror so his full face is visible by reflection.

Assimilating the ubiquitous sexual imagery and the widening legal and social acceptance of homosexuality into his paintings, Currin accordingly paints respectively various pictures of nudes and homosexual interactions. Homosexuality was depicted in Currin's' earlier paintings too. (From the beginning, Currin has never been reluctant to delve into sexuality in all its honest and its compromised dimensions.) In the earlier paintings, homosexual couples were portrayed as attached, affectionate couples in the bourgeois mode. "Homemade Pasta" (1999) has a contented homosexual couple enjoying the ordinary domestic task of making pasta in a kitchen. "Two Guys" (2002) has two homosexuals mingling casually with no sexual overtones. With the two naked men close together on a small rowboat, "Fishermen" (2002) is the painting coming the closest to depicting homosexual sexual encounter. Yet with the two men so busy with rope and net and details of seagull in the sky and catch of fish in the boat, sex if regarded at all, is regarded as an inevitable, not an explicit or expressed subject.

In the 1990's era paintings, sex and also sexuality were one other inevitable or possible subject or theme among other inevitable or possible ones in a Currin painting given its ambiguities and complexities. In the later paintings, however, homosexual sexuality is pronounced. Homosexual sexual images assume a place alongside other sexual imagery.

2. Homosexuality - The Perfection of Autonomous Sexuality

Of the dozen or so paintings of the Gagosian Gallery exhibition, four overtly treat homosexuality. The painting

"Hotpants" (2010) shows two men: one wears thigh-high blue hot pants preening in front of a full-length antique mirror, the other man also wearing hot pants leaning over behind him lifting up the back flap of his matching jacket to get a better look at the blue hot pants. Both men wear knee socks of colors matching the hot pants suit of the other; first man red socks, the man leaning, blue socks. Besides the evident enthusiasm of the two men over the hot pants, the rich setting makes the impression of a special, extraordinary, private, and personal occasion. Additionally, near the top of the painting at the back of the preening figure in blue hot pants, just to the left of the vertical centerline of the painting occupied by the preening one, is a small perfectly circular bubble-like form inexplicably, anomalously, floating in the scene.

This incongruous, perfectly round bubble slightly darker against the pinkish background yet transparent so that it does not blot it out and with a glint of light looking like a star is of the same field of detail--i. e., incongruent detail-- as the incongruities, distortions, and exaggerations of Currin's earlier paintings, and serves the same purpose. The incongruities, although seemingly arbitrary and incidental to the main image, in fact tilt, or inflect, the painting toward statement. They are the true intellectual focal points which though leading at best toward a provisional opinion or interpretation, introduce the direction for such. Thus the empty brick pot held between the elderly couple bent earnestly toward it in a familiar scene of Spring planting in "The Gardeners"; the exaggerated, misshapen rump of the woman in "Stamford After-Brunch"; and in "The Cripple," the discordancy of conspicuous cane for support and breezy smile and tossed hair reveal conflict, withdrawal, and artifice. By contrast, the bubble, the perfect bubble suggests unabashed openness, projection, and wholeness, perhaps completion.

The figures convey as much as well; although without the bubble, the scene would be only a somewhat brash image of homosexuality. Currin would be simultaneously poking fun at the pair for their enthusiasm over the hot pants and unapologetically tendering an elaborate, accomplished image of homosexuality. The bubble however elevates the sex and sexuality dealt with to the plane of magic and fantasy. With the bubble, the preening and peeking of the homosexual pair do not seem so silly or eccentric, but instead in the wider context of magic and fantasy, seem to be acting and playing as necessary to reach or experience the higher plane.

The figure in the blue hot pants preens by jutting forward his pelvis with his feet apart for balance for maximum jutting resembling a thrusting in sexual intercourse. This air of sex is reinforced by the figure in the red hot pants lifting the back flap of the other's jacket to see his buttocks. The jutting stance of the preening one along with the other's lifting of the jacket back flap in a simple, inoffensive conscious act to see the backside of the other suggests that the two are somewhat intoxicated in the aftermath of having just had sex. The bubble could be a champagne bubble. Besides, the men are uninhibited with one another; and their gestures display that although sated, they are prolonging the sexual pleasure as much as possible by their theatrics, probably found to be effective for this in their relationship. But preferring not to leave any ambiguity about the moment pictured, Currin includes a used condom draped over the seat of the antique chair in the lower left foreground. Not wanting to spoil the impression of the magic and fantasy of sex created by the richness of the surroundings and the bubble, the condom, though in the foreground and unmistakable with its shape and bulge of semen at its tip, is drooped over the front of the chair seat so perspective on it is not sharp. It resembles one of Dali's radically distorted, "melted," clocks in his surrealist painting "The Persistence of Memory"; or at first it could be taken for a sock. Sex is in the air. The bubble floats by. The cultural acceptance and openness regarding sex as seen by the prevalence of sexual imagery and lessening stigmatization of homosexuality is smoothly and plainly assimilated into the painting "Hotpants."

3. Voices from Lesbianism

Currin however goes further than he does in "Hotpants" in representing the contemporary regard of sex. The majority of paintings are individuals. But in those smaller number which contain more than one person, all have strong suggestions of sexual relations--homosexual sexual relations specifically--between the persons. And one, "The Women of Franklin Street" (2009), has three early middle-aged women (late 30s, early 40s) engaged in sex. A woman mostly naked except for sheer stockings and a nightgown held around her midriff looks out to the viewer; while to her right a woman wearing a shift tongues her left breast and fondles her hairy vagina, and to her left behind her left shoulder, another woman, naked, leans her right cheek tenderly against the woman's shoulder. The most intriguing feature of this painting is the face of the central woman looking out toward the viewer, especially her expression.

The central woman cannot be unaware of the sexual attentions and acts of the two other women. There is literally sex on all sides of her. Nonetheless, the expression on her face evinces no response to the sexual stimulations being done to her most erogenous parts, nor to the affectionate touch of the cheek of the woman on her shoulder. This central woman, the main figure, is not oblivious nor dismissive of the physical, sexual acts being done to her. Nor is she supercilious actually or make-believe as if taking such ministrations as her right or mocking the hopeful yet insufficient advances of either of the two other women. By her expression, the central woman shows no hint that she is not aware of the situation she is in. He legs are held slightly apart and her pelvis is thrust slightly forward for the vagina fondling of the woman to her left; and her nightgown is lowered so her shoulder is bared for the soft, warm touch of the other woman's cheek. Yet the woman looks out to see if the sexual scene is being observed with not the slightest sign of embarrassment or surprise nor search for envy in the viewer. The most striking point about the middle woman's outward look is that there is nothing striking about it. Imparting neither that the onlooker should be surprised nor that she is surprised at being come upon in the midst of the sexual activity, what her expression imparts mostly is normality. With the culture permeated with sexual imagery so that even legislation and political observance are reflecting the new acceptance and openness, there is nothing for the woman to be surprised or ashamed about, nor for an onlooker either. Currin's "The Women of Franklin Street" is testimony that the culture's new attitudes and mores about sex and sexuality are no longer speculative, tentative, or restricted, but have come to take residence in expectation, judgment, reaction, and other areas of communal life.

Besides "The Women of Franklin Street," two other paintings treat lesbian sexuality. "The Conservatory" (2010) shows two women with faces close to each other's with lips almost touching. One woman is at the back of the other; the closer women who is the main figure in the center twists her head so her face can be close to the other's in the embrace. Both women are mostly naked in only bras and stockings. The breasts of the woman in front are exposed. This woman's right hand clutches the neck and bow of a violin whose body rests on something covered by a crumbled drapery or cover winding through the lower part of the painting. The woman's other hand grips a section of the cover that she holds against the vagina of the other.

In "Dogwood Thieves" (2010), two women stand beside each other in a field in springtime as evidenced by the fair sky and small bit of tawny ground covering in the background, but most notably by the budding dogwood branch held by the woman on the right cutting diagonally across the middle of the painting and in front of the woman of the left. Also, the woman to the left holds a large round straw spring hat trailing a red ribbon over her torso; which one assumes is naked since her shoulders and upper chest below her neck are bare. The woman on the right wears a bra. The fingers of her right hand on the other's right shoulder indicate her arm is across the other's back. What one assumes is a blanket--light gray-blue in color--runs from the left shoulder of the woman on the right down her left arm leaving exposed her bra-covered breasts and her left hand holding the bottom of the dogwood branch; where the blanket then cuts across the lower part of the painting covering the lower part of each woman's body as much as included in the painting (to a little above the knees) which the viewer assumes is naked or scantily clad. As in "Hotpants," the sexual imagery of "Dogwood Thieves" stops short of explicit sexual acts. Nonetheless, while there is no object such as the used condom in "Hotpants," in "Dogwood Thieves" the budding dogwood branch leading from the vagina area of the woman on the right across the breasts of the woman on the left, the embrace of the two woman, and the blanket suggest recent or imminent sexual play between the two woman.

4. Self-Contained Sexuality

Even the paintings where there is only one figure speak to how sexuality and sex have been incorporated into all aspects of contemporary life. In "The Reader" (2010), a pleasant-looking younger, completely naked woman reads a book in her lap. Unselfconsciously absorbed in her reading, she represents how sexuality has entered into the simplest, most common, most familiar, everyday activities; entering into these in such a way that is taken for granted and does not interrupt concentration (similarly to how the woman in "The Woman of Franklin Street" looks calmly out at the viewer as if to illustrate that not even stimulation of her clitoris is affecting her). The woman's reflection in a mirror she is sitting beside and has her right arm propped atop in "The Reader" suggests dimensions reaching to society beyond her solitude as she reads. Another telling touch added by Currin is the gray length of fabric curled around her arm atop the mirror. It could be part of a cover or a garment. There is no reason for it to be curled around her arm--except to imply that in the contemporary ambiance colored by explicit and implicit sexuality, clothing and coverings having been pushed to marginality are discretionary. The concept, consideration, or custom of clothing or covering as a "wrap" for the body is subverted.

Another painting iterating this point about clothing and coverings by positioning such an article at the periphery of a figure is "The Old Fur" (2010). A pink-skinned nude woman (fortyish) sits with her legs pulled toward her on a dark blue surface with a brownish-red drapery behind her. Her torso--especially noticeable at her waist--is thick and disproportionate to her small, dainty legs. Her legs are pulled toward her so her vagina is not visible. Her smallish breasts are visible however, and she seems to be wanting to call attention to them the way they are forward from the way her back is arched and also because they are revealed by her holding open an ermine fur with golden fabric interior across her back. Her arms stretched away from her body to hold the fur open also seem to be positioned as a gesture of introduction for her bared breasts and body, like a master of ceremonies would spread his arms as a welcome to a performer. The rich, full-length ermine fur in fact seems a stage curtain pulled back for the appearance of the breasts. The theatrical connotation of the painting is carried further by the drapery behind the woman, as if it were another part of a stage's curtains. As obviously luxurious as the ermine coat is, it is not it but her average body, especially her breasts, the woman wants to be seen. The fur is not a wrap at all, but rather a backdrop against which to display the nude body, not cover it.

"Mademoiselle" (2009) too has a similar play of nudity and curtain-like elements. Another pink-skinned woman--this one with sharper features and a nicer figure and no distortions--sits with her legs pulled toward her. She sits on a dusky white blanket; and in the background is a red panel and above it a pale green panel. This woman wears a black, transparent negligee that is trimmed with black fur. The negligee is open at the front so that this woman's breasts are visible, as the woman's in "The Old Fur." This woman is casual however. She appears restful. Her eyes are closed; but her head is held up, so it is obvious she is not asleep. Her left arm is comfortably resting on the back of what may be a chair covered by the blanket; and her right arm with four pearl bracelets rests comfortably at the hip of her right leg pulled up to her. The painting is not explicitly, openly sexual, except as a female nude figure inevitably brings this in. But it is more than a study of nudity as is familiar in the field of art. As in "The Old Fur," the theatrical references of the blanket the woman is posed on and the way her fur-edged negligee is open just to the degree that it reveals her breasts and thus frames them connote Currin's consistent, unmistakable theme of the

appearance and status of sex and sexuality running through
his recent paintings.

5. Wringing Out Remnants of Puritanism

Taken as a whole and in relation to the reading of the
1990's paintings as noting strains and artificialities
surfacing in individuals, relationships, and social
interactions from unsettling feelings of change fraying
individuals' sense of innocence crucial to their identity and
sense of wellbeing, Currin's latest paintings convey how the
sense of innocence was kept from being lost, and so was
renewed as it has periodically in American culture.

This was accomplished by the employment of diverse, yet
interrelated characteristics of American culture. The
bourgeois values (as connoted by the luxuriant articles in
the background of some of the paintings), material culture,
marketing techniques, packaging design principles, the
ubiquitous media especially television (e. g., the series
"Desperate Housewives" and frequent sexual scandals such
as those involving Eliot Spitzer and Tiger Woods),
entertainment, the preeminence of popular culture, the
concept of "youth culture," and the transforming power of
art--with Currin's own art works contributing to this--
worked in concert to bring about an essential change in the
place of sex and sexuality. Overall, this change moved
along the lines of commercialization, as various ideas and
materials do in becoming a regular, familiar part of
American culture. Notably with regard to the lines of
commercialization, prostitutes came to be called "sex

workers"; and the concept of "transactional sex" applied not only to prostitutes, but also sexual relations in some marriages and the casual, temporary sexual relations between unmarried men and women. For instance, Eliot Spitzer's relationship with the escort service--e. g., sex ring--which led to his resignation as governor of New York has been called "transactional sex" in trying to explain why he failed to realize that he was placing his political career and reputation in peril. So this explanation goes, seeing himself involved in what was basically a business transaction something like his membership in a tennis club for recreation when he was not at his duties as governor, Spitzer failed to recognize how vulnerable he was leaving himself.

The cultural process of the commercialization of sex and sexuality is not ordinarily explicit as with the terms "sex worker" and "transactional sex" however. And the commercialization need not be explicit to be instrumental, substantive, and effectual. Sex and sexuality associated with products of popular culture has a larger role in the transformation of their place because this is part of everyday experience. In being so, the changing regard of sex and sexuality is readily, usually barely consciously accepted and adopted by the general population. Thus one sees in today's beer commercials during televised sports events men and women with pelvises thrust slightly, nonetheless obviously as meant by the creators of the ad for its audience. Such jutting pelvises in beer commercials are reminiscent of ones in certain paintings of Currin's. In the TV ads, usually the slightly jutting pelvis are on the same visual par as the featured beers or a slightly lower, yet still competing level; as when a beer bottle is held near the jutting pelvis so both can be taken in in the same look, or when a young man or woman waves a beer bottle while simultaneously jutting his or her pelvis in an especially animated larger movement suggesting there is hardly any difference between the beer and sex in satisfying desire. In one beer ad I recall seeing recently, the beer (I can't remember which brand) became almost incidental as the young man (early 20s) who was the main character went wandering off to try to meet pretty, alluringly dressed young women around the bar. The beer was always in view and occasionally prominent as "product placement." This sort of ad demonstrates the advertising approach that sex and sexuality can have equal status in an ad to deliver the message of the desirability of a particular product.

The commercialization is removing from the culture vestiges of Puritanism lingering into postmodernism developing after more than a century of modernism. Secularism has been one of the primary developments of modernism. Nonetheless, the Puritan foundations of the country have continued to be a touchstone and a presence influencing to one degree or another individual morality (as well as political activism, ideas of community and other social fundamentals). The transformative movement to the acceptance and openness of sex and sexuality is among other developments, a movement from the Puritan religious idea and moral principle of innocence and its relation to sex. The Puritan relationship with sex with its powers of temptation was one of constraint and regulation by self-discipline. Although the Puritan's did not believe that such self-discipline would put one in a state of innocence, they did believe that it was necessary for a proper relationship to God. The distortions, incongruities, artifices, and subjects' strained features of Currin's 1990's paintings reflect the shocks to the remains of the Puritan regard of sex and sexuality as they are being removed by the cultural momentum bringing the new relationship to these essentials of human being. Because the moral concept of innocence was bound into the Puritan teachings and practices on sex, the 1990's paintings were also reflecting the figures' concerns that the possibility of any type of or measure of innocence was also being lost.

So long as any vestiges of the Puritan regard of sex and sexuality derived from the prime moral concern of innocence remained in individual psyche or social mores, individuals and social interaction--as portrayed in Currin's 1990's paintings--would be in some degree of conflict with the new, building regard of sex and sexuality being unstoppably ushered in by the media, entertainment, the arts, etc. The resolution for this discomfort could not be reassertion or restoration of the historic Puritan regard of sex and sexuality; which regard was a part of the mentality, judgments, and personal and social behavior going in to the founding of the country. The resolution could be only a new concept of innocence corresponding to the regard of sex and sexuality emptied of any vestiges of the Puritan regard.

Especially, Currin's pictures of homosexuality imply this new regard of sex and sexuality unrelated to the Puritan one of tradition, history, moral orientation, self-discipline, and public display and behavior. Despite the flamboyance, luxuriant settings, and directness of Currin's later paintings of homosexuals, they are not celebrations of homosexuality; nor are they provocations meant to shock sensibilities or move a viewer to at least a recognition and perhaps an acceptance of homosexuality. These later paintings of homosexuality are statements of the new concept of sex and sexuality. The flamboyance, luxuriant settings, and directness token the new status of sex and sexuality as represented by the homosexuals in the paintings. As the luster and openness of the paintings depicts, sex and sexuality have attained the status of an ideal. With their poses and surrounding finery (e. g., drapery, fine furniture), the homosexuals resemble statues in public squares more than individuals engaged in or at the moment even concerned about having sex and giving and receiving pleasure going with this despite the patent sexual overtones of the paintings. And the viewer interacts with the paintings on this basis--i. e., their being like statues--more than to them as paintings picturing the erotic or the sexual.

The paintings with individuals who are not expressly homosexual raise other aspects of the new regard of sex and sexuality not defined in the paintings of homosexuals with their statue-like imagery and implications of this. These other later paintings have women alone in various states of nudity or sexual suggestion. Together, the absence of men in any of the later paintings except for homosexuals and the presence of woman by themselves show how far the new regard of sex and sexuality has moved from the Puritan regard. These two factors of the later paintings taken as a whole show that vestiges of the Puritan regard have been removed so that the new regard now stands on its own no longer causing conflict, confusion, or uneasiness because it was vying with remnants of Puritanism. The new, contemporary regard--the regard a la mode--could not be the ideal as pictured in the homosexual paintings nor whole and independent as pictured in the paintings of women alone unless the Puritan regard had been extinguished.

The commercialization of sex and sexuality per se--which is different from using sex to sell products--similar to how fashion and celebrity have been commercialized in the consumer culture of postmodernism has separated sex and sexuality out of their biological, procreative connotations. This separation occurred inevitably during the extinguishing of the Puritan vestiges attached to sex and sexuality for a principle of the Puritan regard was that sex was primarily for procreation, and the distinct, incomparable pleasures of sex were to insure human beings would always instinctively and naturally procreate for the continuation of Humanity. Thus with the Puritan regard, sex and sexuality were integrated into family life, the purpose of one's existence, the order of the community, and Divinity's creation of Humankind. One's sexuality was completely and finally decided by one being a man or a woman; and one had the simple and stable identity of one or the other. By contrast, these days sexuality has come to be largely taken in by the notion of gender; which notion is complex, multifarious, subject to many individual impulses and fantasies and to cultural influences, and sometimes regarded as arbitrary and provisional.

6. The Return to Eden

The new regard of sex and sexuality emptied of Puritan vestiges is presented not only by the presence of homosexuals (including lesbians) and lone women in Currin's paintings, but by the absence of regular men. More than the presence of the homosexuals and lone women, this absence implies the separation of sex and sexuality from procreation. There are not even any allusions to procreation as being only a desirable or practical repercussion of sex and sexuality. Procreation does not appear in the multiple and varied paintings even to be depicted in a lowered or marginalized status or as a faint remembrance. Sex and sexuality have become self-contained to the exclusion of any vestiges of the Puritan regard even as this grew out of biology, preservation of the species, and other naturalistic scientific principles. The new regard is thus emptied not only of remnants of Puritan morality, assessment, and regulation concerning sex and sexuality, but also naturalistic and scientific considerations and to some degree, intuitions.. Sex and sexuality have become self-contained so that display of these (as in the Currin paintings) sufficiently and ideally provides the satisfactions and probably for many the pleasures of these. Where marriage, offspring, comprehensible and continuous identity, and standing in the community were once outgrowths of the Puritan regard of sex and sexuality, now sex and sexuality are defined by vanity, exhibitionism, sybaritic taste, and minimal concern about privacy.

As sex and sexuality have become more public, the sense of innocence has correspondingly returned and grown. The development of the public presence of sex and sexuality--in advertising, in television and movies, on the Internet in social networking and pornography, in the media, etc.--has been the main way by which innocence has been reformulated for it to find once again and to maintain its part in personal identity, mores, ideals, and other aspects of individuals' psychology and psyche and public, communal cohesion, interaction, and movement.

The presence and acceptance of sex and sexuality has been more than a further step in the visual and material culture and the consumerism of postmodernism; and it has been more than a further burgeoning of the era's hedonism, relativism, and self-centeredness. If the acceptance and presence of the sex and sexuality were a step forward, an essential continuation of primary elements of the visual and more sensuous culture and consumerism of postmodernism, Currin's 1990's paintings would not have reflected such conflict. This conflict was more than temporary confusion or disorientation in a moment of introspection or social setting. Frozen in the distorted features of individuals and incongruous details such as a cigar held backwards against spare backgrounds, the conflict was patently, palpably rooted in something other than, something deeper than this. The conflict was cultural and historical conflict not to be resolved by a mere shrugging off of the mystery of disorientation, the resumption of composure--or the reversing of the cigar.

The resolution of deep, persisting cultural and historical conflict is not a change of mood or a technique for composure, but a reformulation of areas of the culture the conflict is occurring in. As the cultural conflict reflected in Currin's 1990's paintings was the subtle, yet affective sense of the loss of innocence, in relation to the idea of innocence as inhering in and in some ways institutionalized in America's foundations, reformulation of diverse, pervasive areas of the culture was called for with individuals accepting the new formulations--the new appearances--and adapting to them so their conflicts would be resolved.

Although the reformulation entailing sex and sexuality was empty of the Puritan regard of these, it was nonetheless fed by and guided by Christianity. A Christian sect, Puritanism involved the perspective of Humankind as fallen as told in the Bible's Book of Genesis. Self-discipline, adherence to a clear moral code, sharp division between the sexes, and regulation of sexual matters and thus control over them were concordant with the perspective of Humankind as fallen; and the self-discipline, etc., were relevant, important, crucial, and were enforced because by them, individuals were able to come as close to the original state of innocence as was possible in human existence. And the state of innocence individuals were in--and their community was in as a body--was the ground for how close they were to their God. Thus, Puritans were not only austere and serious individually; but, as the trials of reputed witches and the exiling of misfits demonstrate, rigorously meted out punishment for what they took as transgressions jeopardizing individuals' and the community's relationship to God. The new regard of sex and sexuality coming into place in the time of postmodern frivolity, frisson, diversity, self-centeredness, visual culture, and media saturation was divorced from the key religious, moral symbolism of Humankind as fallen as recounted in Book of Genesis. The new regard reflected the characteristics and qualities of postmodernism to the complete exclusion of any remnants or even resonances of the traditional Puritan regard.

The new regard did not however turn from essential Christian religious lore and symbol. The new regard is not paganistic nor pornographic; though it has characteristics of either of these for its apparent glorification and revelry of the physical (the body), for lack of a concept of spirituality, often programmatic character, casualness, commonality (as opposed to privacy), and absence of subtleties and refinements of seduction and the erotic. The paganism and pornography ascribed to the post-Puritan sex and sexuality have to do not with their basic nature, but are responses to and readings of their prevalence, sometimes flagrant display, their commercialization, and the status and interest of these in academia. The post-Puritan regard of sex and sexuality is also often taken as paganistic or pornographic because these seem to go with and are expected in a mostly secularized culture. The essential reference for the new regard of sex and sexuality however, is found beyond its multiplicitous appearances and prevalence.

The reference for the new regard of sex and sexuality is the Garden of Eden. The post-Puritan regard is a pre-Fall regard. Whereas in conjunction with conception of human being as a fallen Humankind, the Puritan regard relegated sex and sexuality to a specialized, differentiated, and somewhat cloistered status as indicated by the self-discipline and the public censures with respect to it, the matter and place of sex and sexuality in the new regard resembles that of the Garden of Eden. The Garden of Eden was a state of being wherein sex and sexuality had no special status, were not differentiated from natural surroundings or among human qualities, and were simply, unthinkingly accepted since they did not stand out in any way.

As the story of the Fall in the Book of Genesis suggests, the first knowledge Adam and Eve gained upon eating the forbidden fruit of the tree of the knowledge of good and evil was the knowledge of sex and sexuality. In the Genesis story, when God first created Adam and Eve, "They were both naked, the man and his wife, and they were not ashamed." (All Bible quotes are from the King James' version.) Upon eating the forbidden fruit, "The eyes of them both were opened, and they knew that they were naked." Realizing they were naked--a concept which had never occurred to them before they acquired knowledge from eating the forbidden fruit--"They sewed fig leaves together, and made themselves aprons" so they would not be ashamed in being naked in front of each other. The crucial significance of Adam and Eve having come to the knowledge that they were naked is emphasized in a closely following passage where "Adam and his wife hid themselves from the presence of the Lord God amongst the trees of the garden" because seeing them wearing fig leaves, God will know they had acquired the knowledge they were naked and with this the related sense of shame, and thus they had undoubtedly eaten the forbidden fruit.

The Genesis story of Adam and Eve's--and by implication all Humankind's--Fall does not explicitly go beyond denotation of nakedness, a feeling of shame when realizing one is naked, covering up nakedness, and avoiding an encounter with another where questions concerning one's newly-awakened awareness of the concept of nakedness and recently devised garb to cover it up would arise. Specifics of the Genesis story of the Fall, as spare as these are, singularly bring in matters of sex and sexuality that are entailed in Humankind's fall from grace and expulsion from the paradise of the Garden of Eden into a world of travails and ills. Passages coming right after God sees Adam and Eve clothed in the fig leaves expand on this relationship between sex and sexuality as being involved in the expulsion from Eden. God tells Eve, "I will greatly multiply thy sorrow and thy conception, in sorrow thou shalt bring forth children..."; and to Adam, God says, "[C]ursed is the ground for thy sake."

Before sending them from Eden, God clothed Adam and Eve in "coats of skins." The play of nakedness and being clothed; of being ashamed and remedying this; of detecting awareness of nakedness and the shame going with being naked in front of another; what this awareness of nakedness may disclose about one's sense of guilt; and how one's sense of being naked affects one's relationship with another are all implicated in the brief Genesis tale of the Fall. Returning to the state of being before the Fall puts all of these problematic, troublesome, unsettling, mercurial, and unpredictable elements out of human life and relationships. Without the presence and play of these brought on by awareness of nakedness, one enjoys the simplicity, security, and comfort of paradise.

7. The End of Shame

With their treatment of sex and sexuality mostly fragmentarily, implicitly, and satirically in the early paintings and repetitively explicitly and holistically in the later paintings, Currin's paintings trace the psychic and sociological process by which a likeness of the pre-Fall, Edenic state came into being in the culture.

The primary end of this process--necessary for it to succeed--was eliminating feelings of being ashamed by being naked in front of another and also any implications of guilt or disobedience to any customs, conventions, or laws (such as God's commandment not to eat the forbidden fruit) attached to being clothed to cover one's nakedness. The way for this end to be accomplished is to do away with the concept of nakedness. The tale of Adam and Eve in the Garden of Eden distinguishes their unawareness of any such matter as nakedness as the prime attribute of their existence in paradise. The unawareness of nakedness is seen as the prime, if not the sole qualification for their being able to exist in paradise. Once they lose this unawareness, once they become aware of nakedness, they are no longer qualified for paradise--and thus are banished from it.

In the Bible, whose morality and imagery are at the

foundation of Western culture, unawareness of nakedness is a sign of primordial innocence. The movement from unawareness of nakedness to awareness of nakedness is a movement from innocence to the loss of innocence. Primordial innocence is approached by attempting to become unaware of nakedness. This is impossible: But culture--particularly modernist, postmodern culture with its extravaganza of amusements, sense of mischievousness, and intent to abolish traditions and depart from norms--has subterfuges, artifices, amnesia, and social pressures for the formulation of particular states of mind. Such devices all stem from the absence of authority, and are attempts to create a semblance of it. Unawareness of nakedness is a state of mind contemporary, early twenty-first century culture works to inculcate. Such unawareness is measured in degrees and reflected in a great variety of ways; which measurements and ways include indifference, familiarity, expectation, and resignation. Currin's recent, early twenty-first century paintings present a variety of imagery of the new, pre-Fall, Edenic regard of nakedness. The figures of the paintings reflect varied aspects of this new regard; while in sorting out one's feelings regarding the varied imagery of nakedness as represented by the figures and clarifying one's thinking regarding the imagery, one develops the new regard of nakedness.

The major, decisive step in the formulating presence of the Edenic, paradisiacal regard of nakedness is the step of nakedness from transgressive to everyday. When nakedness loses it transgressive power--its power to shock, upset, or annoy--the culture has shifted to a paradisiacal state. The cultural sign that this has occurred is the prevalence of nakedness and stages and facsimiles of it. (A stage of nakedness is dresses with see-through parts; a facsimile is body-clinging clothing.) Because of nakedness's association with innocence as specified in the Book of Genesis, the regard of nakedness is key to the sense of innocence. And because of nakedness's power of sexual stimulation in developed culture, nakedness has to be separated from sex and sexuality as much as possible. This is what Currin does in his recent paintings by putting nakedness on display in settings with more than one individual and also only one individual. Sex and sexuality are seen to be changing across the entire range of cultural situations, from individuals' regard of their own sexuality and familiarity with it to sex and sexuality's presence and influence in interaction with others.

Such devices all stem from modernism's aspiration to abolish authority. With respect to Adam and Eve's being ashamed in the Garden of Eden, they were ashamed because of the presence of God. Their hiding among the trees to attempt to avoid encountering God when they heard him approaching because they knew they were naked and had covered themselves is an explicit image of the relationship between authority and awareness of nakedness. The presence of God also figured into Adam and Eve being ashamed before each other when they became aware they were naked after eating the forbidden fruit. They became aware of their nakedness and felt ashamed because they had eaten the fruit which God had forbidden them to. They were ashamed in front of each other because they knew individually and mutually that they had disobeyed God. If there had been no God, there would have been no matter of a forbidden fruit or command not to eat it; and Adam and Eve would not have come to know they were naked. The relationship is plain: No authority, no awareness of nakedness; no commandment, no boundary to transgress; no transgression, no being ashamed. Currin's later paintings announce that this classic relationship between authority and shame has been effectively dissolved in contemporary culture.

With its excessive subjectivism, postmodernism has banished authority, as God banished Adam and Eve. In so doing, the primordial innocence enjoyed by Adam and Eve in the Garden of Eden was embraced as this is maximally and optimally possible in existence. In such a world of nature, human being, conflict, and death, the innocence is not--and cannot be--the pure innocence of Adam and Eve in the Garden of Eden before their Fall. Nonetheless, the banishment of authority, in demonstrating human faculties, widening the scope of freedom, and strengthening the spell of dreams and fantasies, also makes innocence, eternally desirable and obsessively sought, seem immediate. In the absence of authority, the state of childhood blossoms. It is not the mindless, emotionally autonomous state of infancy however and early childhood. It is a resemblance of the state of childhood charged with adolescent and adult fantasies (mostly sexual fantasies, which are the strongest and continual), bourgeois notions of pleasure, consumerism, and the mercurial meretriciousness of popular culture. In such a culture, narcissism forms to give a center for the diversity and bring qualities of human being to it to give its primary elements value, if only the value of pleasure. Narcissism fills the vacuum left by the banishment of authority in postmodernism. By its sense of universal entitlement concomitantly effacing particulars in an essentially undifferentiating desire where action is shaped by impulse and reflex rather than selection or reflection, narcissism is a version of unawareness. It is not the perfect unawareness of the Garden of Eden--where the concept of self or awareness of death is impossible, for example--yet the postmodern narcissism is instrumental in generating and sustaining the Eden-like atmosphere awash with imagery, sensations, and ideas of sex and sexuality.

Since the association between nakedness and sex and sexuality is so strong and seemingly natural--like a stigmatization--when looking at a later Currin painting, the theme of sex and sexuality cannot help but come to mind and feelings going with sex and sexuality cannot help but be aroused. But the concepts and feelings are not ordinary or fixed--and this is enough to assert the point that nakedness is not tied to sex and sexuality as conventionally, customarily taken to be. The more one reflects on one's aroused thoughts and feelings, the more one realizes that the traditional, post-Fall regard of sex and sexuality is weak and faded. The power of nakedness over traditional, post-Fall ideas of sex and sexuality is shattered. In Currin's paintings in the 2010 exhibition, the post-Fall regard of sex and sexuality have not been completely eliminated, as they cannot be. In the style of the paintings and one's interaction with them, one however encounters the process by which the post-Fall regard is being minimized as much as possible by prevalence, variations, repetition, and ubiquity working interconnectedly in a process of familiarization. Maximum familiarization as both presence in the public space and psychological and emotional accommodation (e. g., as expectation, absence of criticism) would correspond with the best sense of innocence attainable.

The end of the process of familiarization is not the taken-for-granted attitude toward the varied and constant instances of sex and sexuality, as an indication of an "open," "sophisticated," or "youth-oriented" society for example. For the familiarization alone would leave the process inconsequential, the nakedness meaningless, the sex and sexuality abstractions. The purpose of the familiarization and the end of it is a freshened, felt, Edenic, pre-Fall sense of innocence. The image of such a sense of innocence as the best sense of innocence attainable would be Adam and Eve in the Garden of Eden before having eaten the forbidden fruit. Adam and Eve were naked, and they were not ashamed. Hence, as Currins's paintings present, by the process of familiarization, modern-day, early twenty-first century culture moves to a new realm of sex and sexuality where meeting with their prime and in many ways exclusive representation, nakedness no longer evokes a sense of feeling ashamed.